THE ELEMENTS

Platinum

Ian Wood

BENCHMARK BOOKS

MARSHALL CAVENDISH
NEW YORK

Benchmark Books
Marshall Cavendish
99 White Plains Road
Tarrytown, New York 10591

www.marshallcavendish.com

Library of Congress Cataloging-in-Publication Data

Wood, Ian, 1946–
Platinum / Ian Wood.
p.   cm. — (The elements)
Summary: Examines the discovery of platinum, its chemical make-up,
its uses, and its importance in our lives.
ISBN 0-7614-1550-5
1. Platinum—Juvenile literature. [1. Platinum.] I. Title. II.
Series: Elements (Benchmark Books)
QD181.P8W662004
546'.645—dc21   2003051986

Printed in China

Picture credits
Front Cover: Johnson Matthey plc
Back Cover: Johnson Matthey plc

Corbis: James L. Amos 24, Tim Graham 23 (*top*)
IBM: 21 (*top*)
David K. Joyce: 9
Johnson Matthey plc: *i, iii,* 4, 5, 7, 8 (*bottom*), 10, 11, 12 (*top*), 12 (*center*), 13, 14, 15, 19, 20,
21 (*bottom*), 22, 23 (*bottom*), 25, 26, 27 (*bottom*)
National Library of Medicine: 8 (*top*), 17
Schott Glass Ltd.: 18
Science Photo Library: 27 (*center*), Malcolm Fielding/Johnson Matthey plc 30,
Astrid & Hanns-Frieder Michler 16

Series created by The Brown Reference Group plc
Designed by Sarah Williams
www.brownreference.com

Contents

What is platinum?

Platinum is an extremely dense, silvery white precious metal. One of the main uses of platinum is to make jewelry and other decorative items. Platinum is considered to be more precious than gold, because it is much more expensive to produce pure platinum.

Platinum is also an important metal in industry. Around one quarter of all the goods made in factories worldwide either contain platinum or are made by using the metal in some way. The industrial uses of platinum range from helping to make glass and electronic components to coating the magnetic disks of computer hard drives. Many automobile parts contain platinum. Spark plugs and the electronics of engine control, airbags, and braking systems all contain platinum. It also helps to reduce automobile pollution by cleaning up exhaust fumes.

Platinum does not react with air, water, or most other chemicals, so it resists corrosion. It is also a good conductor of electricity. Both of these properties make platinum ideal for use in electronic medical implants—devices fitted

Bars and nuggets of pure platinum metal. Deposits of platinum are found in tiny amounts in Earth's crust and only in a few parts of the world.

Inside the periodic table

Platinum (chemical symbol Pt) is the heaviest of a group of six metals called the platinum group metals. The other platinum group metals are iridium (Ir), osmium (Os), palladium (Pd), rhodium (Rh), and ruthenium (Ru). If you look at the periodic table of chemical elements at the end of this book, you will find ruthenium, rhodium, and palladium in the second series of transition metals, before

inside peoples' bodies. These devices include pacemakers that keep hearts beating regularly and ear implants that help people hear better.

Platinum can withstand very high temperatures, so the metal is often used to make containers that hold molten substances. This platinum crucible and stirrer are used in the glassmaking industry.

silver. Osmium, iridium, and platinum are in the third series of transition metals, before gold.

Inside the atom

Everything in the universe is made up of tiny particles called atoms. Atoms contain even smaller particles called protons, neutrons, and electrons. Protons have a positive electrical charge, electrons have a negative electrical charge, and neutrons are neutral—they have no charge at all. Protons and neutrons cluster together at the dense center, or nucleus, of an atom. The electrons revolve around the nucleus in a series of layers called electron shells.

Chemists give each element an atomic number so they know how many protons and electrons its atoms contain. Platinum's atomic number is 78, so each atom contains 78 protons and 78 electrons. The protons and neutrons combine to give an atom its mass. Platinum has an atomic mass of 195, so it contains 117 neutrons.

PLATINUM ATOM

Nucleus

First shell
Second shell
Third shell

Fourth shell
Fifth shell
Sixth shell

The number of protons in the nucleus of an atom matches the number of electrons revolving around the nucleus. Each platinum atom has 78 protons in its nucleus and 78 electrons revolving around the nucleus. The electrons spin around in platinum's 6 electron shells. There are 2 electrons in the inner shell, 8 in the second shell, 18 in the third shell, 32 in the fourth shell, 17 in the fifth shell, and 1 in the outer, or valence, shell.

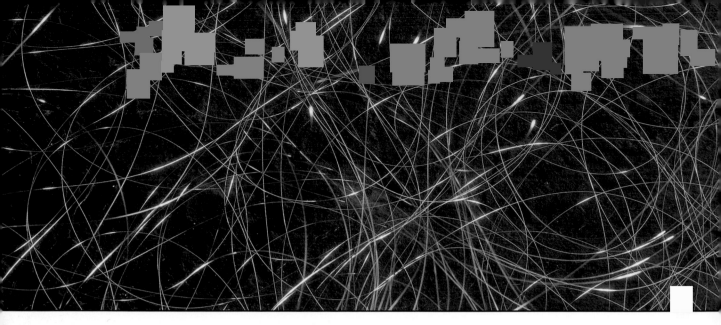

Special characteristics

Platinum is so ductile that just a fraction of an ounce of the metal will stretch into a wire thinner than a human hair and more than 1 mile (1.6 km) long.

Platinum is one of the densest materials on Earth. Density is a measure of the mass of a given volume of a substance. The density of platinum is 12⅖ ounces per cubic inch (21.45 g/cm³). By comparison, lead has a density of just 6½ ounces per cubic inch (11.35 g/cm³).

Although platinum is dense, it is relatively soft. Jewelers can shape it into intricate patterns because it is very malleable (easily hammered or rolled into shapes) and highly ductile (easily drawn out into fine wires or threads).

Chemical properties

Platinum is a very unreactive metal. It resists corrosion by water, oxygen in the air, and most other chemicals—even at very high temperatures. In fact, the only substance that can dissolve platinum is aqua regia—a mixture of concentrated nitric acid (HNO_3) and concentrated hydrochloric acid (HCl). This reaction is used to separate platinum from its ores.

PLATINUM FACTS	
Chemical symbol	Pt
Atomic number	78
Melting point	3,216 °F (1,769 °C)
Boiling point	6,921 °F (3,827 °C)
Density	12⅖ ounces per cubic inch (21.45 g/cm³)
Number of isotopes	Six natural isotopes (around forty artificial isotopes)
Name's origin	The word *platinum* comes from the Spanish *platina del Pinto,* which means "little silver of the Pinto River"

The discovery of platinum

People first began to use platinum about 2,000 years ago in Egypt and South America. The Europeans did not find out about platinum until the sixteenth century, when the Spanish began their conquest of South America. While searching for gold, Spanish conquistadors found heavy lumps of an unknown metal. They called the metal *platina del Pinto,* meaning "little silver of the Pinto River." They gave it this name because they found a lot of platinum in the sands of the Pinto River in Colombia.

The Spanish took some of the samples back to Europe. In 1557, Italian–French scientist Julius Caesar Scaliger (1484–1558) analyzed the samples. He found that the mystery metal was not silver but a completely new metal.

This picture shows the platinum chalice presented to Pope Pius VI in 1788.

European chemists forgot about the new metal for nearly two hundred years. Then, in 1735, Spanish scientist Antonio de Ulloa (1716–1795) rediscovered platinum in South America. He returned to Europe in 1745 with a few samples for scientific study. De Ulloa's rediscovery marked the beginning of platinum's popularity as a decorative metal. In 1783, French chemist François Chabaneau (1754–1842) discovered how to purify platinum. In 1788, some of Chabaneau's platinum was shaped into a chalice for Pope Pius VI (1717–1799). By the end of the nineteenth century, platinum was in great demand for jewelry and a number of industrial uses.

Where platinum is found

Platinum is an extremely rare metal and makes up just a tiny fraction of all the material in Earth's crust. Most of the platinum deposits in the world are located in just a few areas of southern Africa, Russia, North America, and South America. Some of this platinum is in the form of lumps of the metal. These range in size from small grains to large nuggets weighing up to 20 pounds (9 kg) or more. Sometimes the metal lumps are almost pure platinum. These are known as native platinum deposits. More often, platinum is alloyed (blended) with other metals, including other platinum group metals and copper, gold, iron, and nickel.

Native platinum and platinum alloys are found in beds of sand or gravel in rivers or buried under the ground. The sand or gravel and the platinum come from old rocks that have been eroded (worn away) over millions of years by water, wind, and ice. Platinum deposits of this type are known as placer deposits.

Another source of platinum is in ores— platinum compounds found inside rocks in the ground. Some platinum ores include sperrylite (platinum arsenide; $PtAs_2$) and cooperite (platinum sulfide; PtS). Small amounts of these ores are often found inside rocks containing the ores of other metals such as copper and nickel. When the ores are refined (turned into pure metals), the platinum is obtained as a by-product.

A sample of the platinum ore sperrylite taken from the Stillwater Complex in Montana.

PLATINUM FACTS

LEADING PRODUCERS

In 2001, the leading platinum producers were

South Africa	140.6 tons (128 tonnes)
Russia	44.6 tons (40.5 tonnes)
North America	12 tons (11 tonnes)
Rest of the world	3.8 tons (3.4 tonnes)

Platinum producers

More than 70 percent of the world's supply of platinum comes from southern Africa. The Bushveld Complex in the Transvaal region of South Africa is the largest platinum mine in the world. It contains over 75 percent of the world's platinum deposits. The Bushveld Complex also contains about 50 percent of the world's supply of palladium and large reserves of metals such as chromium and vanadium.

Russia is the next biggest platinum producer. Russian mines in the Norilsk-Talnakh region of Siberia produce around 20 percent of the world's platinum supply. Six percent of the world's platinum comes from North America, where there are large deposits in Alaska, Montana, and Ontario, Canada.

Platinum also comes from a number of other countries all over the world. Some of the main producers include Australia, Brazil, Colombia, Finland, Indonesia, Ireland, Japan, Madagascar, New Zealand, Peru, and Zimbabwe.

The Stillwater Complex in Montana is one of the most productive platinum mines in the United States.

Mining and refining

Getting platinum from placer deposits is relatively simple. Machines dredge up the platinum-bearing sand or gravel from riverbeds or dig it out of open pits. Then the sand or gravel is washed away and the nuggets of platinum are purified.

Mining platinum ores

Some platinum ores come from open-pit mines, but most deposits are buried deep underground. In an underground mine,

A worker packs explosives into mineral-rich rock buried deep underground at the Bushveld Complex in South Africa. Underground mining is hard and dangerous work for the miners.

miners drill long holes deep into the mineral-rich rock using hand-held pneumatic (air-powered) drills. Then they pack explosives into the holes and blast the rock to pieces. Machines collect the broken rock and haul it to the surface of the mine for processing.

Processing platinum ores

Refining platinum ores (to get the pure metal) can be a long, difficult, and costly process. It can take up to six months to process a batch of ore, and it takes up to 12 tons (11 tonnes) of ore to produce just one ounce of platinum.

At the surface of the mine, workers crush the mineral-rich rock into small particles and mix them with water and chemicals. This separates the platinum

Flotation separation concentrates platinum minerals from the rock in which they are found. Workers mix crushed mineral-rich rock with water and chemicals. Machines then blow air through the mixture. The bubbles created carry the mineral particles to the surface of the mixture where they are skimmed off.

minerals from the rock. Air blown through the mixture creates bubbles that carry the mineral particles to the surface of the liquid. The bubbles create a froth rich in platinum minerals. Workers skim off the froth and dry it to form a concentrated powder. Each ton of powder contains between 3 and 30 ounces (85 and 850 grams) of platinum group metals (PGMs).

DID YOU KNOW?

TESTING THE ORE

Platinum mining is expensive, so people need to see if there is enough metal in the ore before they start digging. This process is called assaying. Assayers treat a small sample of the ore with heat and chemicals to dissolve the metals. Then they use a machine called a spectroscope to measure how much platinum is in the sample.

Next, the powdered minerals are heated to over 2,732 °F (1,500 °C) in an electric furnace to remove any impurities. When these impurities have been removed, air is then blown through the "matte" of minerals that is left. Oxygen in the air removes any iron and sulfur in the matte. The PGM content of the matte is now more than 50 ounces (1.4 kg) per ton.

Platinum reactions

Further processing removes any base (common) metals such as copper and nickel. This leaves a material containing

A worker pours pure molten platinum metal into a crucible ready for casting into ingots.

---

15 to 20 percent of PGMs—mostly platinum alloyed with gold. The final stage involves treating the material with chemicals to get pure platinum.

Platinum producers use aqua regia to dissolve the metal from the mineral concentrate. Aqua regia is three parts concentrated hydrochloric acid (HCl) and one part concentrated nitric acid (HNO_3). Platinum will not dissolve in either of these acids alone, but when they are mixed, chlorine is released from the hydrochloric acid. The chlorine, together with hydrogen from each acid, combines with platinum to form chloroplatinic acid (H_2PtCl_6). A chemical called ammonium chloride (NH_4Cl) then converts the chloroplatinic acid to fine particles of ammonium hexachloroplatinate ($[NH_4]_2PtCl_6$). This is filtered out and purified and burned to produce pure platinum metal.

The platinum group metals

Grains of silvery white palladium—an important catalyst in the automobile and petroleum industries.

In 1802, a British scientist called William Wollaston (1766–1828) was doing some experiments with the waste materials left behind after he had purified a sample of platinum. To his surprise, Wollaston found that the waste materials contained a completely unknown metal. He called this new metal palladium in honor of Pallas—the ancient Greek goddess of wisdom. Palladium was the second of the six PGMs to be discovered. Iridium, osmium, and rhodium followed in 1804. Ruthenium was discovered forty years later in 1844.

Palladium

Palladium is a silvery white metal with an atomic number of 46. This metal has a density of 6%₀ ounces per cubic inch (12.02 g/cm^3) and melts at a temperature of 2,826 °F (1,552 °C). Like all the PGMs, palladium does not react with many chemicals, so it resists corrosion.

Palladium jewelry is very popular, but this metal has many other important uses. Catalysts are materials that speed up chemical reactions or help chemicals react with one another. Palladium catalysts are widely used in the petroleum industry. They also help to clean up the toxic gases from automobile exhausts. Palladium is also used to store hydrogen gas safely. The metal can absorb up to 900 times its own volume of hydrogen at room temperature, then release it again when it is heated.

Iridium

Iridium is a shiny, yellowish white metal with an atomic number of 77. This PGM has a density of 13$\frac{1}{10}$ ounces per cubic inch (22.7 g/cm^3), making it the second densest element on Earth. Iridium is very hard but brittle. It melts at 4,429 °F (2,443 °C). It is highly resistant to corrosion—more so than any other metal. The high melting point and resistance to corrosion make iridium a very useful metal in industry. An alloy containing platinum and iridium is used to make medical implants such as heart pacemakers.

Pure iridium is a shiny, silvery metal with a very high melting point. It is often alloyed with other PGMs to make crucibles for use in industry.

DID YOU KNOW?

DINOSAUR KILLER

Many people think that the dinosaurs died out when a massive asteroid slammed into Earth around 65 million years ago. All over the world, layers of rock dating back to this time contain a lot of iridium. The iridium levels in these rocks are thousands of times higher than most rocks. This iridium may have come from the asteroid that killed off the dinosaurs.

Iridium is the rarest of all the PGMs. It takes its name from the Latin word *iridis,* which means "rainbow." One of the scientists who discovered iridium, British chemist Smithson Tennant (1761–1815), gave the metal this name because it forms brightly colored compounds.

Police detectives use osmium tetroxide (OsO_4), dissolved in water to stain fingerprints. This compound binds to traces of skin grease in the fingerprints. It stains the grease dark brown or black, which makes the fingerprints visible.

Osmium

Osmium is the hardest of the PGMs and, at 13 ounces per cubic inch ($22.6 \ g/cm^3$), is the densest material in the world. Osmium has an atomic number of 76 and melts at a temperature of 5,481 °F (3,027 °C). This bluish white metal takes its name from the Greek word *osme,* which means "odor," because osmium tetroxide has a strong, chlorinelike smell.

Like palladium, osmium is used as a catalyst, and its hardness makes it an ideal wear-resistant coating for the parts of fountain pens and electrical contacts.

Rhodium

Rhodium is a silvery white metal with an atomic number of 45. This PGM has a density of 7⁷⁄₁₀ ounces per cubic inch ($12.41 \ g/cm^3$) and melts at a temperature of 3,571 °F (1,966 °C). Rhodium takes its name from the Greek word *rhodon,* which means "rose," because some of its compounds are rose-colored. The main use of rhodium is as a catalyst, especially in the catalytic converters of automobiles.

Because it is very hard and resistant to high temperatures and corrosion, rhodium is used in the production of nitric acid (HNO_3). It is also useful in the glassmaking industry. Many silver goods are coated with a thin layer of rhodium to prevent the silver from tarnishing.

Ruthenium

Ruthenium is a hard, white metal with an atomic number of 44. This PGM has a density of 7⅕ ounces per cubic inch ($12.37 \ g/cm^3$) and melts at a temperature of 4,082 °F (2,250 °C). Ruthenium takes its name from the word *Ruthenia*—the old name for Russia—because it was discovered in a sample of platinum ore found in Russia.

Ruthenium is often used as a catalyst. Iridium-ruthenium catalysts help to make acetic acid (CH_3COOH) from methanol

DISCOVERERS

PGM PIONEERS

The discovery of the PGMs began in 1802, when British chemist William Wollaston (1766–1828) isolated and identified palladium. Two years later, Wollaston discovered rhodium. Around this time, British chemist Smithson Tennant (1761–1815) discovered iridium and osmium. Tennant was helped in his work by the research of French chemists Nicolas-Louis Vauquelin (1763–1829) and Antoine de Fourcroy (1755–1809). In 1827, Swedish chemist Jöns Jacob Berzelius (1779–1848) and his German colleague Gottfried Osann (1797–1866) separated ruthenium oxide from platinum ore. Berzelius and Osann could not turn the oxide into pure ruthenium, so they sent a sample of the oxide to a friend—a Russian chemist called Karl Karlovich Klaus (1796–1864). Klaus successfully isolated pure ruthenium from this sample in 1844.

A portrait of William Wollaston, the British chemist who discovered palladium and rhodium.

(CH_3OH) and carbon dioxide (CO_2). Many common household products, such as adhesives, cleaning liquids, and paints, contain acetic acid. Ruthenium is used to coat equipment in factories that make corrosive chemicals. It is also alloyed with other metals to make them harder.

Platinum group alloys

Platinum is the most abundant PGM. Other PGMs occur in smaller quantities, and in nature are almost always found alloyed with native platinum and in platinum ores. The PGMs are separated when the platinum is refined. PGMs also appear in the ores of copper and nickel. They are also produced as a by-product when copper and nickel are refined.

There are some naturally occurring platinum group alloys. One example is an alloy called polyxene, which contains up to 90 percent platinum plus iron, other PGMs, copper, gold, and silver. Platiridium is a rare alloy of platinum and iridium. Osmiridium contains osmium and iridium plus small amounts of platinum, rhodium, and ruthenium.

Platinum and its alloys

L ike gold, platinum is a "noble" metal. Unlike base metals such as copper and iron, noble metals do not react with many other chemicals. Iron corrodes very quickly when it comes into contact with moist air. The water and oxygen in the air combine with iron to form a compound called rust (iron oxide; Fe_2O_3). Rust starts off as a thin film on the surface of the iron, but it quickly spreads through the metal. Noble metals stay bright and shiny. They do not react with water or oxygen in the air, even when they are heated in a white-hot flame. They also resist the corrosive effects of most acids.

Since platinum resists attack by corrosive chemicals and can withstand very high temperatures, it is a vital part of modern technology. In laboratories and factories, platinum helps scientists and manufacturers handle dangerous materials

One way platinum is used is to manufacture high-quality glass. Temperature-resistant platinum alloys are used to make vessels to hold molten glass.

PLATINUM FACTS

PLATINUM USES
The percentage of world platinum production used by different industries:

●	Jewelry	51
●	Automobile	21
●	Electrical/Electronic	7
●	Chemical	6
●	Glass	4
●	Coins and ingots	3
●	Petroleum	2
●	Other industries	6

safely. And platinum-based components are used in all sorts of high-tech gadgetry, from the magnetic disks of computer hard drives to jet engines and rockets.

Platinum alloys

Pure platinum is used for some of these applications, but for many of them platinum alloys are best. Alloys are mixtures of two or more metals, or sometimes a metal and a nonmetal such as carbon. Alloys are designed to have desirable characteristics. For example, adding ruthenium to platinum makes a very hard alloy—much harder than either platinum or ruthenium alone.

Uses of platinum alloys

Scientists heat materials to very high temperatures in crucibles (small pots) made of platinum alloyed with iridium.

They put the crucibles into furnaces heated by gas flames or by an electric current flowing through a platinum wire. Platinum crucibles are used to make semiconductor crystals for the electronics industry and the crystals that produce laser light. In a laser, an intense pulse of normal light bounces around inside the crystal and emerges as a laser beam.

People working with materials at high temperatures need to know exactly how hot they are. Conventional thermometers are useless for measuring thousand-degree temperatures because they would melt. High-temperature thermometers produce electrical signals that change as the temperature changes. One type uses a thermocouple to measure temperature. This electrical device contains an alloy of platinum and rhodium and can measure temperatures up to 1,800 °F (3,270 °C). Factories making materials such as steel use thermometers with platinum alloy thermocouples to monitor the temperature of the molten materials.

In the glassmaking industry, the raw materials used to make some types of high-quality glass for television tubes and

DID YOU KNOW?

PLATINUM EAGLES

The U.S. Mint produces a range of platinum coins called American Platinum Eagles. People buy these coins as an investment, hoping to sell them later at a profit. The 1-ounce Eagle has a face value of $100—the highest of any U.S. coin ever minted.

flatscreen computer monitors are melted in vessels made of platinum alloys. The paddles that mix and stir the materials are also made of platinum alloys. To make the thin threads of glass used in fiber optics, molten glass is forced through nozzles called spinnerets, which are also made of platinum alloys.

Platinum alloys often replace gold for plating connectors and switch contacts in electrical and electronic equipment. Platinum alloys are more durable than gold, and they resist damage by electrical sparks. Automobiles also use platinum alloys in the electronics that control the braking and engine-management systems and in the mechanisms that trigger the airbags.

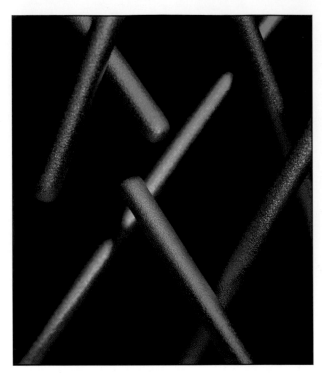

Thermocouples coated with an alloy of platinum and iridium are used to monitor the temperature of molten materials such as glass and steel.

Magnetic platinum

Adding tiny amounts of the metal cobalt to platinum gives the resulting alloy magnetic properties. The magnetic disks of more than 90 percent of computer hard drives are now coated with this platinum alloy. The platinum-cobalt magnetic coating allows the disks to store more data than older coatings could manage.

Jets, rockets, and missiles

Platinum alloys are very strong, so they are ideal for use in jets and rocket engines. Not only do parts of these engines get very hot, they also have to withstand the corrosive effects of burning fuel and hot gases. The nozzles that spray the fuel into jets are often made of platinum alloys. Platinum alloys would be good materials for the fast-rotating turbine blades, but these alloys are very expensive to produce.

DID YOU KNOW?

PLATINUM AT WAR

During World War II (1939–1945), the U.S. government banned the manufacture of platinum jewelry so that the metal could be used to make military equipment such as spark plugs for warplane engines.

DID YOU KNOW?

PLATINUM PHOTOGRAPHY

With ordinary black-and-white photographic prints, the image is formed by reactions involving silver compounds. Over time, these compounds break down, and the images slowly fade. In platinum photography, images are formed by reactions involving platinum, palladium, and iridium compounds. These compounds are very stable, so the images take longer to fade.

The largest single use for platinum in the electronics industry is in the production of the magnetic coatings for the disks of computer hard drives.

However, platinum may soon be used to make turbine blades as well as fuel nozzles. Scientists are now developing nickel-based "superalloys," which contain fewer PGMs and are cheaper to produce. These alloys will allow engineers to make turbine blades that work at high temperatures. Engines with these blades will burn their fuel more efficiently and cause less pollution. Since the engines will be working at much higher temperatures, the new superalloys will also be used to make components other than the turbine blades.

A thin coating of platinum alloys is also used to protect the nosecones of some missiles as they fly through the air at supersonic speeds.

In space, platinum alloys are used to make small rocket motors that move satellites into orbit once they separate from the launcher rockets. Some rocket motors can also change the position of the satellites once they are in orbit.

Other applications

Platinum and its alloys have many other important uses. They are made into coins and jewelry, dental implants, and even parts for musical instruments such as flutes. Some flutes are made almost entirely of pure platinum. The flutes are expensive—they can cost $25,000 each—but the density of the platinum gives the flutes a distinctive tone.

Platinum alloys resist spark and heat damage, so they are used in the tips of spark plugs of automobile engines.

A decorative metal

Jewelers shape platinum washers into shiny rings and set them with gemstones such as diamonds.

The use of platinum for jewelry and other decorative items has been popular in Europe since the late eighteenth century. The first platinum jewelers had no way to shape the metal into elaborate designs, so the range of platinum jewelry was limited. Early jewelers melted the metal in furnaces and then poured the molten liquid into molds and hammered and cut it into shape as it cooled and solidified. But they did not have the technology to pull the metal into fine wires and form intricate shapes.

Toward the end of the nineteenth century, the invention of high-temperature blowtorches and new shaping techniques gave jewelers a quick and easy way of heating platinum and fashioning it into decorative designs. Platinum jewelry and ornaments flooded the market, and these items became an instant success with wealthy people in Europe and the United States. Famous jewelers such as Tiffany & Co. in New York and Cartier in France worked hard to keep up with the demand for this popular metal.

Modern jewelry

Today, the single largest use of platinum is still for making decorative jewelry. Many people prefer the color of platinum to that

---

DID YOU KNOW?

WHITE GOLD

In Japan, platinum is called *hakkin,* which means "white gold." In other countries, white gold is the name given to a white-colored gold alloy, which contains other metals such as nickel, zinc, and smaller amounts of platinum or palladium.

of gold. Over 40 percent of engagement and wedding rings sold in the United States are now made of platinum.

Platinum and diamonds

Some people think that gold jewelry makes diamonds look yellow and dulls the diamond's natural brilliance. Silver does not alter a diamond's color, but it is a very soft metal. Jewelers must set diamonds in a large amount of silver to keep the gemstones secure, so silver jewelry set with diamonds is often large and heavy. Platinum does not alter the color of a diamond, and it is stronger than silver. As a result, platinum jewelry set with diamonds is sturdier, lighter, and more delicate than

DID YOU KNOW?

PLATINUM CROWN
The jewel collection of the British monarchy includes a magnificent crown made of pure platinum metal. This crown is set with 2,800 gems and includes the Koh-i-noor diamond—one of the biggest diamonds in the world.

Platinum is particularly good for holding diamonds and other precious gemstones.

diamond-studded silver jewelry. Some of the world's biggest and most expensive diamonds have been set in platinum.

Alloyed jewelry

Most platinum jewelry is made of alloys rather than the pure metal. Palladium makes platinum softer, so it is easier to shape into chains and wires. Platinum is often coated with rhodium to make the jewelry shinier. To coat the platinum, the jewelry is first put into a liquid containing rhodium compounds. An electric current passes through the jewelry. This makes the rhodium in the liquid settle as a thin layer over the platinum jewelry.

Platinum catalysts

Every year the platinum group metals are used to make millions of tons of important chemicals. They do this by acting as catalysts—substances that speed up reactions without themselves getting chemically altered during the reaction.

Acid production

Acids are very important chemicals in industry. They are used to make products such as detergents, explosives, fertilizers, medicines, and plastics. PGM catalysts play a vital part in the production of many different acids. Nitric acid (HNO_3) production begins by passing a mixture of ammonia gas (NH_3) and oxygen gas (O_2) over a red-hot gauze made of 90 percent platinum and 10 percent rhodium. The ammonia and oxygen gases first form nitric oxide (NO) and then nitrogen dioxide (NO_2). The nitrogen dioxide dissolves in water to form nitric acid.

Workers install a platinum-rhodium gauze, which acts as a catalyst in the production of nitric acid.

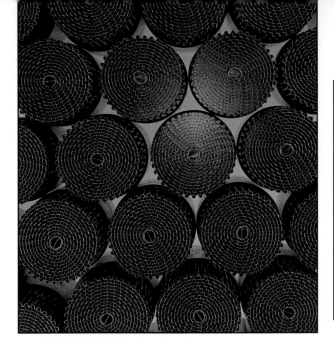

These catalytic converters are used to break down the harmful gases in automobile exhaust fumes.

Catalytic converters

An automobile engine gets its power by burning a mixture of air and gasoline. When this mixture burns, it turns into a mixture of gases such as nitrogen oxides and carbon monoxide. These gases pass from the engine into the car's exhaust system. Nitrogen oxides and carbon monoxide are pollutants—dangerous chemicals that harm the environment.

Modern automobile exhaust systems contain catalytic converters to convert the pollutants into harmless chemicals. PGMs are the catalysts in catalytic converters. They trigger reactions that break down nitrogen oxides into nitrogen and oxygen. This oxygen combines with the carbon monoxide to make carbon dioxide. The oxygen also combines with unburned fuel to form water and more carbon dioxide.

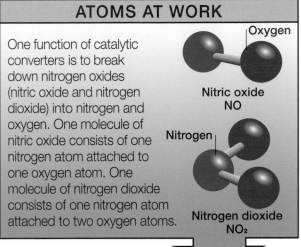

ATOMS AT WORK

One function of catalytic converters is to break down nitrogen oxides (nitric oxide and nitrogen dioxide) into nitrogen and oxygen. One molecule of nitric oxide consists of one nitrogen atom attached to one oxygen atom. One molecule of nitrogen dioxide consists of one nitrogen atom attached to two oxygen atoms.

Oxygen

Nitric oxide
NO

Nitrogen

Nitrogen dioxide
NO₂

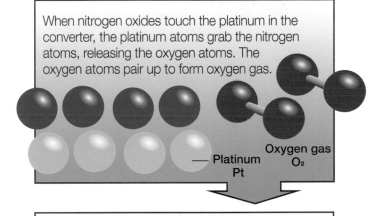

When nitrogen oxides touch the platinum in the converter, the platinum atoms grab the nitrogen atoms, releasing the oxygen atoms. The oxygen atoms pair up to form oxygen gas.

Platinum
Pt

Oxygen gas
O₂

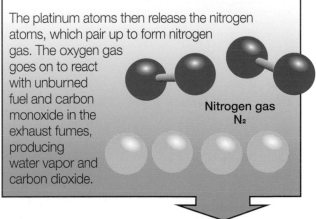

The platinum atoms then release the nitrogen atoms, which pair up to form nitrogen gas. The oxygen gas goes on to react with unburned fuel and carbon monoxide in the exhaust fumes, producing water vapor and carbon dioxide.

Nitrogen gas
N₂

The chemical reactions that change nitrogen oxides into nitrogen gas and oxygen gas are written like this:

$$2NO \rightarrow N_2 + O_2$$
$$2NO_2 \rightarrow N_2 + 2O_2$$

Platinum in medicine

Platinum group metals and platinum alloys have many valuable uses in modern medicine. For example, they are used to make surgical instruments and medical implants. New drugs based on platinum compounds also help in the fight against some cancers.

Platinum implants

Unlike other metals, PGMs do not react with the tissues and fluids inside peoples' bodies to create harmful substances. This makes them very safe to use as medical implants. For example, they are used as dental fittings to rebuild damaged teeth. PGMs are also good conductors of electricity, so they make good electrodes (electrical contacts) for implanted devices such as pacemakers. Pacemakers produce electrical signals that keep hearts beating regularly. Platinum-iridium electrodes deliver these signals to the person's heart.

Aural and retinal implants also use platinum-iridium electrodes to deliver electrical signals in the body. Aural implants work like tiny hearing aids. Surgeons insert them inside the ears of deaf people to help them hear sounds again. Retinal implants are light-detecting devices that fit inside the eye. They might one day help some blind people see again.

Neural implants may someday help the victims of Parkinson's disease. People affected by this brain disorder find it hard to control their muscles, and their limbs tremble constantly. Neural implants could deliver electrical signals into the brain through platinum-iridium electrodes. These signals would help to reduce the muscle tremble caused by Parkinson's disease.

Platinum drugs

One of the most recent uses for platinum in medicine is in the development of new drugs. Drugs based on the platinum compounds cisplatin (Platinol®) and carboplatin (Paraplatin®) help doctors treat a wide range of cancers, including those of the bladder, ovaries, and testicles.

All the cells in the human body grow by dividing over and over again. Tumors develop in areas where body cells divide

DID YOU KNOW?

BETTER BLOOD FLOW

Surgeons often insert tiny tubes called stents into blood vessels to stop them from closing up and blocking the blood flow. These stents consist of a platinum-iridium wire mesh. These metals are unreactive, so the body does not reject the stents.

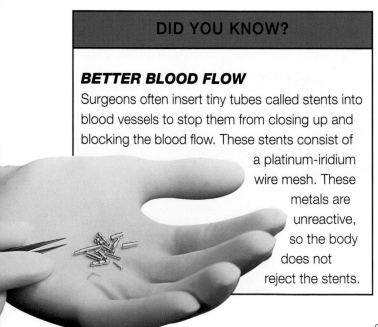

also have their drawbacks. Unpleasant side effects include loss of balance, pain in the joints, and swollen legs and feet. Since these drugs interfere with cell division, they may also stop healthy body cells from dividing. Unfortunately, treatment with platinum-containing drugs can trigger the development of other cancers such as leukemia (cancer of the tissues that make blood cells).

too quickly. Platinum-containing drugs work by stopping these cells from dividing. Eventually, the cancer cells die away. Cisplatin and carboplatin may be effective cancer treatments, but they also

Platinum-containing drugs such as Paraplatin® and Platinol® are used to treat some types of cancer.

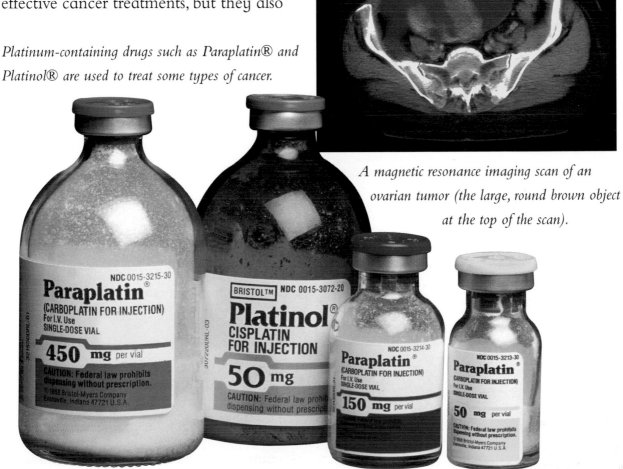

A magnetic resonance imaging scan of an ovarian tumor (the large, round brown object at the top of the scan).

Periodic table

verything in the universe consists of combinations of substances called elements. Elements consist of tiny atoms, which are too small to see. Atoms are the building blocks of matter.

The character of an atom depends on how many even tinier particles called protons there are in its center, or nucleus. An element's atomic number is the same as the number of its protons.

Scientists have found around 110 different elements. About 90 elements occur naturally on Earth. The rest have been made in laboratories.

All the chemical elements are set out on a chart called the periodic table. This lists all the elements in order according to their atomic number.

The elements at the left of the table are metals. Those at the right are nonmetals. Between the metals and the nonmetals are the metalloids, which sometimes act like metals and sometimes like nonmetals.

- On the left of the table are the alkali metals. These elements have just one electron in their outer shells.

- On the right of the periodic table are the noble gases. These elements have full outer shells.

- Elements in the same group have the same number of electrons in their outer shells.

- Elements get more reactive as you go down a group.

- The number of electrons orbiting the nucleus increases down each group.

- The transition metals are in the middle of the table, between Groups II and III.

Transition metals

Group I

Group II

1 H Hydrogen 1									
3 Li Lithium 7	4 Be Beryllium 9								
11 Na Sodium 23	12 Mg Magnesium 24								
19 K Potassium 39	20 Ca Calcium 40	21 Sc Scandium 45	22 Ti Titanium 48	23 V Vanadium 51	24 Cr Chromium 52	25 Mn Manganese 55	26 Fe Iron 56	27 Co Cobalt 59
37 Rb Rubidium 85	38 Sr Strontium 88	39 Y Yttrium 89	40 Zr Zirconium 91	41 Nb Niobium 93	42 Mo Molybdenum 96	43 Tc Technetium (98)	44 Ru Ruthenium 101	45 Rh Rhodium 103
55 Cs Cesium 133	56 Ba Barium 137	71 Lu Lutetium 175	72 Hf Hafnium 179	73 Ta Tantalum 181	74 W Tungsten 184	75 Re Rhenium 186	76 Os Osmium 190	77 Ir Iridium 192
87 Fr Francium 223	88 Ra Radium 226	103 Lr Lawrencium (260)	104 Unq Unnilquadium (261)	105 Unp Unnilpentium (262)	106 Unh Unnilhexium (263)	107 Uns Unnilseptium (?)	108 Uno Unniloctium (?)	109 Une Unilenium (?)

Lanthanide elements

Actinide elements

57 La Lanthanum 139	58 Ce Cerium 140	59 Pr Praseodymium 141	60 Nd Neodymium 144	61 Pm Promethium (145)
89 Ac Actinium 227	90 Th Thorium 232	91 Pa Protactinium 231	92 U Uranium 238	93 Np Neptunium (237)

The horizontal rows of the table are called periods. As you go across a period, the atomic number increases by one from each element to the next. The vertical columns are called groups. Elements get heavier as you go down a group. All the elements in a group have the same number of electrons in their outer shells. This means they react in similar ways.

The transition metals fall between Groups II and III. Their electron shells fill up in an unusual way. The lanthanide elements and the actinide elements are set apart from the main table to make it easier to read. All the lanthanide elements and the actinide elements are quite rare.

Platinum in the table

Platinum has atomic number 79. It belongs to a group of elements called the transition metals. Like most other metals, platinum is a good conductor of electricity and heat. Unlike most other metals, it does not react with many other elements. Platinum is extremely valuable. It is used to make jewelry and other ornamental items.

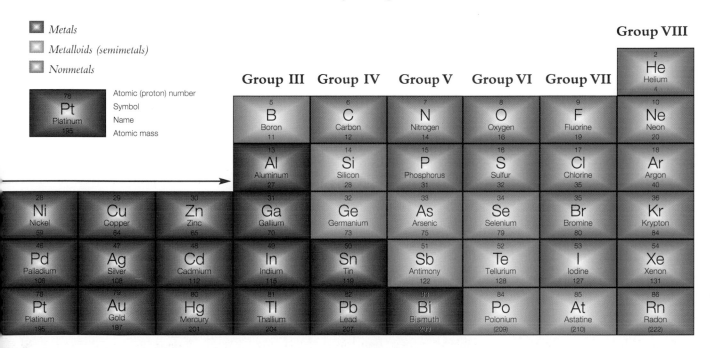

Chemical reactions

Chemical reactions are going on all the time—candles burn, nails rust, and food is digested. Some reactions involve just two substances, others many more. But whenever a reaction takes place, at least one substance is changed.

In a chemical reaction, the atoms do not change. An oxygen atom remains an oxygen atom; a hydrogen atom remains a hydrogen atom. But the atoms join together in different combinations to form new molecules.

A man holds up a large circular gauze made from woven platinum-rhodium wire. The gauze is used as a catalyst to produce nitric acid from ammonia.

Platinum chemistry

Platinum is very unusual because it is so unreactive. Unlike most metals, platinum does not react with pure acids to form salts. It also resists attack by strong alkaline solutions. Platinum will form compounds with other elements under certain conditions. But these compounds are not very stable and easily break down to form the pure metal again.

A more stable way of getting platinum to combine with other elements is in the form of an alloy. Alloys of platinum are mixtures of platinum with other metals, often platinum group metals.

Platinum and some platinum alloys act as catalysts. Platinum catalysts help to speed up chemical reactions involving other elements, but they do not take part in the reaction themselves.

Glossary

alloy: A mixture of a metal with another element, often another metal.

aqua regia: One of the only substances that can dissolve pure platinum. It consists of a mixture of three parts nitric acid to one part hydrochloric acid.

atom: The smallest part of an element having all the properties of that element.

atomic mass: The number of protons and neutrons in an atom.

atomic number: The number of protons in an atom.

bond: The attraction between two atoms, or ions, that holds them together.

catalyst: Something that makes a chemical reaction occur more quickly.

compound: A substance made of atoms of more than one element.

conductor: A substance that lets electricity or heat flow through it easily.

corrosion: The eating away of a material by reaction with other chemicals, often oxygen and moisture in the air.

ductile: A ductile material is one that can be stretched easily.

electron: A tiny particle with a negative charge. Electrons are found inside atoms, where they move around the nucleus in layers called electron shells.

element: A substance that is made from only one type of atom.

ion: A particle of an element similar to an atom but carrying an additional negative or positive electrical charge.

isotopes: Atoms of an element with the same number of protons and electrons but different numbers of neutrons.

malleable: Malleable materials can be easily worked into shapes.

metal: An element on the left-hand side of the periodic table.

molecule: A particle that contains atoms held together by chemical bonds.

neutron: A tiny particle with no electrical charge. Neutrons are found in the nucleus of almost every atom.

nucleus: The dense structure at the center of an atom.

ores: Rocks that contain compounds or elements as they are found in their natural form on Earth.

periodic table: A chart containing all the chemical elements laid out in order of their atomic number.

placer deposits: Loose chunks of platinum in sand or gravel.

proton: A tiny particle with a positive charge. Protons are found inside the nucleus of an atom.

refining: An industrial process that frees elements, such as metals, from impurities or unwanted material.

transition metals: The group of metals that forms a block in the middle of the periodic table.

Index

ML   6/04